Calls from the Outside World

Other Books by Robert Hershon

The German Lunatic
Into a Punchline: Poems 1984 – 1994
How to Ride on the Woodlawn Express
The Public Hug: New and Selected Poems
A Blue Shovel
Rocks and Chairs
Little Red Wagon Painted Blue
Grocery Lists
4-Telling (with Emmett Jarrett, Dick Lourie, Marge Piercy)
Atlantic Avenue
Swans Loving Bears Burning the Melting Deer

Calls from the Outside World

Robert Hershon

Hanging Loose Press
Brooklyn, New York

Published by Hanging Loose Press, 231 Wyckoff Street, Brooklyn, NY 11217-2208. All rights reserved. No part of this book may be reproduced without the publisher's written permission, except for brief quotations in reviews.

Printed in the United States of America
10 9 8 7 6 5 4 3 2 1

Hanging Loose Press thanks the Literature Program of the New York State Council on the Arts for a grant in support of the publication of this book.

Cover art and author photo by Elizabeth Hershon
Cover design by Marie Carter

Acknowledgments: Some of these poems first appeared in these publications: *American Poetry Review, Arshile, Boog Lit, The Brooklyn Rail, Greetings, Hanging Loose, Lungfull!, Michigan Quarterly Review, MOMA: The Museum of Modern Art, New Review of Literature, The North, Ploughshares, Poetry Northwest, Plum Line, Saint Ann's Review, Skanky Possum*, and *The World.* "Sentimental Moment" appeared in *Poetry 180* (Random House) and Poetry in Motion (Dallas).

Library of Congress Cataloging-in-Publication Data available on request

ISBN: 1-931236-57-7 (paperback)
ISBN: 1-931236-58-5 (cloth)

Produced at The Print Center, Inc. 225 Varick St., New York, NY 10014, a non-profit facility for literary and arts-related publications. (212) 206-8465

Table of Contents

For Donna & Elizabeth & Jed

For Dick & Marie & Mark

Calls from the Outside World

Celeste called work to leave a message
for Nathan. "Tell him Celeste called.
Tell him *something happened*"

And that became a famous phone message
and part of the folklore
finally working its way into a byword at the
shop and it came to designate a
call from anyone's spouse or
companion   Hey Richie, line six –
something

And there was an amused pride in
having invented such a good piece of
workplace slang, so specialized and so secret
and so site-specific

but before long Nate was gone and then
one by one nearly everybody else
so today the slang is just as good as ever
but completely forgotten or unknown
to the present staff

So we see that for slang to survive
we require a body of speakers
initiated in its use
large enough to provide continuity
and with a core of permanence

This must be why the linguists
invented prisons, as language laboratories
so that the whole country can imitate
the speech of young black men but
never actually have to see them, so white
golfers can cry *You the man*
and little blonde girls can shout
You go, girl

Chicken Suit

A man in a chicken suit
stands at the subway exit
handing out flyers and loudly
proclaiming the virtues of
honey-fried wings or money-
back onion rings
It's hard to understand him
through the plastic beak and
what does a man in a chicken suit
really have to say to you anyway
This assumes it's always the same
man inside the chicken suit but
it might be a new guy every day
unless he is dedicated to this form
a career in a chicken suit
And I have been watching him
from the third floor window
for half an hour now
which may indicate the level
of my own ambition this morning
The eagle suit lies on a chair
waiting for a smart breeze

Messiah on Varick Street

A man in a gray suit
eats his lunch in Sounds of Brazil
He seems to be an ordinary citizen
until the light catches his earring
and makes it dazzle
But wait—
he isn't wearing an earring
It's a narrow ray of sunshine
through the blinds
that catches his lobe
He leans back:
beauty mark on the cheek
Forward to the soup:
mad light in his eye
Now it dances on the wall
just above his head, crying
This one, this one!
It's the sign from heaven
all America awaits
Divinity! Take my life,
my wife, my wide-eyed babies!
I will run home to get you
my life savings
Until then—
please take my watch

A Pressure-Sensitive Label

At eye-level above the urinal
a small printed sign (11-point Helvetica)
on pressure-sensitive stock says
By reading this, you have licked my balls.

If so, it was an amazingly unmoving experience,
bringing neither pleasure nor repugnance,
and it is instantly clear that
the writer's preoccupation is not
with forceful sexual commands—fuck this suck that—
or even with the gentler daydream of testiculingus,
but with exploring the magic of cause and effect,
the twistiness of the tongue outweighing its
simpler functions and leading to more subtle,
layered graffiti, which can plug into a variety of systems.
Christian: This is my body. Lick it.
New York Mets: These are my balls. Bobble them.
Tyson: I can lick any balls in the house.
Elmer's Glue: If you can't lick 'em, join 'em.
Ugly Stepsisters: Have a ball.
Board of Ed: How will this affect reading scores?

Cowpokes, Cavaliers, Stallions in their stalls,
does the writer watch the peruser perusing? By reading this
commentary, you have turned the guns to glass.
By retreating from the urinal, you have in passing
invented the platform heel, made it snow in Rio,
deaccessioned a Caravaggio and more to the point

impaled an innocent party on a coat hook.
Your wet footprints will never dry, leading the police
to the door marked Hombres. Ah, señor, Lieutentant
Rodriguez smiles coldly, by choking back your tears
you do not win the Alaskan cruise and the box of Mars bars.
By dipping your brush in the bucket, you have earned
a lifetime behind these impregnable walls.
Adios, sucker. Reading privileges revoked.

Sylvie

Sylvie and I were telling jokes. Late afternoon, the sun slanting across Market Street, the other reporters had gone home. She was new to the office staff, young and wide-eyed, fresh from London, and she'd been having the usual English-American misunder-standings over lift and lorry and biro and hoover and rubber and it had gotten a bit more troublesome when she'd said to Harry, "Do you mind if I ask how much you screw a week?" meaning how much money do you make. Now it was her turn to top my story about the guy with red balls and the guy with green balls. She was still catching her breath from laughing—it's a really good joke—and she wanted to be sure I'd understand the slang in her punchline. She asked, in some doubt, "Do you know what the word *fuck* means?" I can't remember what joke she told.

My Passage through Grub Street

What luck, Marcella, to hook on as an editor
of *Dog World* after *Cats* magazine folded!
But take care—this might lead you to the
editorship of *Modern Salamander* or
Today's Hippo and when you try for the job
at *Hammer and Tongs Journal,* they'll say
Sorry, but you're in the bow-wow trades,
you couldn't write about fire and steel.
I speak as the former editor-in-chief of
Hosiery and Underwear Review. I once knew
more about socks than almost anybody and if
you'd known me in those days, you would have
received the occasional package with a dozen
pair of argyles in assorted sizes. I used to bundle up
the samples and just send them to everyone I knew.
But not underwear. Underwear, you were on your own.
And you probably shouldn't try this with puppies.
Maybe little packages of Alpo would be okay.
After writing for *Footwear News* and
Women's Wear Daily and *Intimate Apparel*
I cried: enough! I was looking at the bras
instead of the models. Enough! I quit my job,
I left my wife, I sold my kids, I burned down
the house. I transformed myself into the wild,
unpredictable devil I am today, quite likely to
run barefoot through any assembly, master of
the silent tap dance, my lifetime supply of white
crew socks thrown to the four winds and rising to

the clouds! Actually, I took a job writing
speeches. Say, I don't know how you do it,
the speechgiver would say, it sounds just like me.
But it didn't, it sounded just like *me*, except for the
god bless thises and the god bless thats.
So I figured I'd better keep moving before
I *did* sound just like him and I gave up
writing for money and started writing poems
for bits of red ribbon and chunks of blue glass,
fine ribbon, shining glass.

Co-Editors

I was going to write a poem for
your memorial service, about how damned
dark the stairs at Reed Street are.
Why didn't you ever fix that? With tears
in my eyes, I'm holding on for dear life.

I haven't got time to write the poem because
I'm half-buried in your ancient paper, all the old
invoices and statements and credit memos,
all the 3 x 5 cards with pencil scratches. Bob
Cratchit could slip behind this desk and
never miss a stroke.

But you loved to hide behind
this inky wall. If somehow we were having this service
but you were still alive, there's no doubt you'd
have stayed home, licking stamps, puffing smoke,
and letting the cats answer the phone. You'll like the
Ron Schreiber Light Bulb Fund. You can keep
all the records and do the screwing-in.

The Deuce by the Coat Rack

You cannot befriend the waiter
even if you call him Phillip
and ask if his daughter is better
even if he greets you more
or less by name and remembers
that you favor the more modest merlots.
He is on his feet and you are a chair.

When he passes through the swinging
doors into the black kitchen
where a perpetual cigarette smolders
in a tin ashtray just for him,
he has standing and you are a number.

When you pass him on the street
in an entirely different neighborhood
his cold eyes betray no recognition.
On the snowy corner,
he steps around the abandoned chair and
crosses where he pleases.

Illusions of Paradise

Crystal will be your server
said the maitre d'

(And silver my mount to glory!)

Not a Chain

In the restaurant at the end of the world
the waiters continue to serve
and they still accept credit cards

Some people tip everything they have
and others invent complaints so
they won't have to tip a nickel
and can take it all with them

I start to piss in a corner but
I reconsider and zip up
Can we hope all the diners
maintain such standards?

Monday night was pot roast
Tuesday surf and turf
Tonight fire and flood
And they had just learned
to make a decent martini

International Incidents

1.

Wang Ping asks if
we went to a seder
last night
      She did,
in Minneapolis
No, I say, we're not
observant
as though we constantly
overlook details

2.

The teachers in the lounge
crowd around the
Swedish visitor
You must be very proud
one of them beams
to be Swedish
She has no idea
what that means
She says,
I don't *dislike*
being Swedish

3.

Who's ever met a Bulgarian?
he would shout in the bar
Then one night
two homely blond sisters
smiled and said
We are Bulgarians!
They smiled for two weeks
then went away forever

The Remaining Balance

Sometimes, as you know,
a unique talent may go unremarked
by one's peers because of their failure
to perceive or their reluctance to applaud
A case in point is my uncanny ability to balance
this flat triangular stone (the long side measuring
nearly two inches) on top of this dried twig (easily
four inches high) planted in the sand,
lit by long fingers of afternoon sun,
the tiny table supporting two white pebbles, one gray
pebble and—that's enough. People nearby, wearing
the funny hats of the literate rich at ease, affect
not to notice, as we did not notice Mrs. Onassis
in the drugstore in Vineyard Haven (tissues,
sun-block, two prescriptions, something in a pink box)

In the Anxious Asp, on a silent night in medieval San Francisco
drinking beer from a thick mug which distorted
the view from inside, I balanced quarters
on their edges on the bar—
two, three, the ultimate challenge of a dime—
then looked up to see people all along the bar,
balancing quarters. Or trying to. Not everyone
has the talent. Some have it and lose it. Some have it
and leave it in the sun too long. I had it then,
I've got it now. I await the perfect application.

Mysteries of Country Life Explained

Chicken breasts
are grown in fields, they wave
bonelessly in the breeze

Peas in pods were invented in 1922
by a Green Bay engineer
Before that they fell loose
from the sky

Pork chops are chopped
from the tender top branches
of slender white trees

The square white tomato was
developed for efficient shipping
but why white?

Touch a cow on the forehead and
it will instantly break down into
pre-cut sections, pre-wrapped pre-priced
pre-digested pre-eliminated and
growing right back up again
in the meadow

Eggs bubble up from mountain streams
each wrapped in an argyle sock

The night is full of green blood
and gray moths as big as you are
who think your head is a source of light

Oh, the Shelburne Hotel, I Thought You Said Swinburne

Sherman, I thought maybe
you only stayed in hotels
named after poets

At the Hotel Frost
an old man in the back of
the closet
sets fire to your shirts

At the Hotel Williams
the beds never get made because
the doctor is diddling the
chambermaid

You have reservations
at both the Byron and the
Wordsworth, depending on
how you feel about
your sister

At the Hotel Eliot
chapel is compulsory
but don't worry,
Indians and Jews don't
get that far

So go to the Hotel Ginsberg
The sheets are a bit hairy but
room service will bring you
amazing delights, all with bells
and songs

A Short History of World War II

for Terence Winch

I suppose that I will never
be acknowledged as the true
inventor of the Woody Woodpecker
laugh. Even at the age of eight, when
I figured out how the laugh might have
traveled from its birthplace, a chalked-in
punchball diamond on Menahan Street,
by itinerant children

> (but who were these
> homeless wanderers? Not the Quinn brothers
> or Marty Nadler. They must have come from
> another block, showed up once, stole the laugh,
> then headed for the sunset)

until some Brooklyn
ragamuffin fell in with, say, the son of Walter
Lantz and,

> no doubt trying to curry favor with
> that golden child as they sat by the pool—
> young Lantz purring in the sun, actually,
> tattered Brooklyn bargaining from a discreet
> distance, willing to trade anything, anything
> for a nod from the blue-eyed citizenry—

gave away the secret of the laugh,
the million-dollar laugh
that oily young Lantz immediately rushed
to his father's studio, where executives
soon announced a major breakthrough in the
field of triumphant avian laughter
and that's how history records it: with

many a we-surmise and we-must-conclude,
and would-it-not-have-been-logical, ignoring
the missing diaries, the disputed letters, the
strange disappearance of every witness from
Menahan Street a mere sixty years later.
And even then, rounding second, when
I usually died at first, even in that moment
I knew I would forever be denied
justice.

Ross Bagdasarian

In Rosemary Clooney's obituary
there is a reference to her big hit *Come on-a My House*
which is put forth as an example of the terrible shit she had
to sing before she broke through to quality stuff, but
I don't remember it as such a bad song. When I was a kid,
I was impressed that the lyrics were written by William
Saroyan and his cousin Ross Bagdasarian but I didn't know
then that I would remember the name Ross Bagdasarian for
40 years or so even though I never heard it again until I saw it
in Rosemary Clooney's obituary and also learned that he changed
his name to David Seville and founded the Chipmunks, so maybe
even he forgot the name Ross Bagdasarian. And when I was a
          teenager
I never expected to have any connection with William Saroyan
          but now
Aram Saroyan occasionally e-mails political jokes to me
and I remember reading once that he was up
for the part that Dustin Hoffman got in *The Graduate*,
which was the first movie I ever saw in an airplane, flying from
          Seattle
to New York. The movie opens on a tight close-up of Benjamin.
          You can't
tell he's on an airplane, so when you hear the captain's voice
saying that they're approaching Los Angeles, it's very confusing
because you don't know
it's the movie captain, you think it's the real captain and you
          wonder why
the hell the plane has been diverted and why they didn't think to
          mention

it until now and who do I know in Los Angeles and how long
      will I be there.
A whole new life may beckon, a life of glamour and music,
      hanging out with
Rosie and Ross and various singing rodents (Are chipmunks
      rodents? Look that up. Somebody.)
It would beat two days in Seattle, driving around in
      the drizzle
with a superstitious cold canvasser testing a sales talk I wrote.
Stop the car! he'd shout,
yellow house, I can always make a sale in a yellow house. And
      Cooper, he could sell
anyone named Cooper. How about Hooper, I asked. Yeah, yeah,
      Hooper's pretty
good, too, but Cooper is a lock. It was a two-syllable world.
      Come on-a my house,
my house, I'm gonna give-a you Easta-egg.

The Marx Brothers Leave Paramount and Sign with MGM

But Irving Thalberg only wants Groucho and
Harpo and Chico. No room for Zeppo.

Now Zeppo will never be funny. He's got
no costume, no character, no gimmick, and now
he's got no hope. Zeppo will never be funny.

Feeling so damned Zeppo, it gets Zeppo so
early these days, Zeppoing so hard the gutters
overflow, on the road to Gummo.

1960, In Memoriam, the Times Theater, Stockton Street, Now a Chinese Market

for Ed Woods

I was going to walk out the back door of the theater
before the lights came on again but
thought I'd stay for the coming attractions, forgetting
for the moment that there are never coming attractions
at the Times Theater, just Two Action Hits Daily,
more like retreating attractions—Bomba the Jungle Boy movies
and Tarzan jungle movies and Chips Rafferty Australian
jungle movies, George Montgomery westerns and
Lash La Rue westerns and Bill Boyd westerns and
Tex Ritter westerns and it's only twenty five cents if
you get in before noon, carrying yourself very carefully
and sitting as far as possible from the other students of film,
fathers and brothers though they may be. For your convenience,
the men's room is just to the left of the screen, so there is
a constant silhouette parade of short men in wide fedoras
crossing and re-crossing the screen to transact their commerce,
the only movement in the theater except for the striking of matches.
It's too early to go to Gino & Carlo's and too late for Gabby Hayes
to reach the ranch. All choices are grainy.

If luck holds, the fog rolls in early and we are spared the insult
of sunshine. The bar is only a block away, so we can sit like
perfect little gentlemen until those who happen to be working start
straggling in, ready to buy a beer or two, as, god knows,
we would do for them if our positions were reversed. We can tell
them how Randolph Scott turned Albert Dekker over to the sheriff
instead of shooting the son of a bitch. Code of the West and all
that, movie house etiquette and bar etiquette. You can't leave after the

house buys a round. You can't fall off a stool. Take the fight outside.
Maybe you'd feel better if you'd stayed for the newsreel, but there
       is no
news at the Times Theater and no news in the bar. Daffy Duck
is more likely to show up in one than the other.

All this because you called this morning. Well, it was morning
here in the East.

Two New Kids on the Block and One Old One

1.

Omar bounced
over 400 consecutive
times on his pogo
stick, which he thought
might be a new
world's record or
at least a Wyckoff St.
record. He had to stop
because he threw up.

2.

When Anouk was two and
playing on her front stoop
and I came slumping by
at five o'clock, she would
ask if I could stay outside
and play, but it never
worked out. Now she's
four and has many social
responsibilities, so I'll never
know the secret game. We
can still discuss the news.

3.

Benny waited for Jed
in the hall not far from my desk.
He asked me if I was a mailman.
No, I said, why do you ask me that?
Oh, I asked Jed what you do and
he said you "make mail."
So that's what I've been doing
for 30 years since, making mail.
And I just took a minute off
to write this down.

Three Photographs Taken around the House at the Request of Anselm Berrigan and Tom Devaney for a Mysterious Future Project

1. Front Door

This is my house. I have a picture taken of it sixty years ago.
There was no light in front, no towering plane tree at the curb, no
bars on the window. And no Chinese takeout menu stuck in the
door. Why not? Were there no Chinese restaurants in Brooklyn?
Did Seth Low not have a yen for sautéed snow pea leaves at his
desk? Did Whitman not crave an egg roll or two? Or maybe the
First Amendment rights hadn't been firmly established yet. Today,
we proudly exercise that freedom: dinner on the table in fifteen
minutes and free Cokes, too.

2. Helen Adam's Stones

Toward the end, Helen was convinced that she was going to
jail. Then, she said, all her beloved books and pictures and *objets
d'art* would be thrown in the trash. And there were many books
and pictures and objects, so many that you couldn't spread your
arms and turn in a circle without knocking several things down.
Nothing could shake Helen's belief that prison was waiting, even
when I pointed out that a woman in her eighties could prob-
ably commit murder and not serve a day. But she thought she
had made a mistake in some Medicaid papers "and you know,
Bob, that's a *federal* crime." So each time I left her apartment, she
would press one of her prized polished stones on me, so it would
have a loving home. We played that scene six times and six stones
now sit on the mantel, guarded by Lizzie's sort-of-Peruvian figure,

a staunch defender even though she may actually be a cookie jar. Helen never went to jail, but when she left the apartment for a nursing home a few years later, everything she owned was taken away by lawyers.

3. Trash

The streams that once flowed through New York have all been covered over and the hills have been flattened and the Singer Building and the Old Post Office and Penn Station have been torn down, but there are new urban pleasures. Such as black plastic garbage bags. Here we see a structurally arranged group, with dazzling silver highlights provided by the afternoon sun. On wet days, the bags form innumerable little craters which fill with rainwater and reflect the gray sky, with each fleeting bird repeated over and over. At night, the massed shape might be a Claes Old-enburg Volkswagen. Or a slouching beast. Or a thousand pounds of mashed potatoes. Say, it's like living in a gallery! And I haven't even conjectured on what my neighbors have put *into* those bags. Did one just move?

Neighbors

The conversation consisting of
thud and fuck you
Something heavy hits the wall
A picture shifts
Fuck *you*, she shouts, *fuck* you

A dish or a glass. No, a bottle.
Fuck you, she shouts, you motherfucker,
you fucking motherfucker, fuck you

I want to reach through the wall with
an armload of sharpened intensifiers—
You mongoose bowel, you cabinet of phlegm,
you guppy-hearted elbow pipe—
so that, if when she bleeds, the Red Sea,
she can end the refrain, thrust home

But does it matter what she shouts,
but that she shouts, against thud
and push, any words, any arithmetic
One fuck you plus one fuck you
is one fuck you   Some days, I suppose,
only the classics will do

The Sun Never Sets on Sunset Park

One morning the Italian dockworkers
and the Scandinavian sailors had all
shaped up or shipped out and Sunset Park
was Brooklyn's new Chinatown
with bins of frogs and eels on 8th Ave.
Some crippled survivors of past civilizations
remained on the side of the road—
a Studebaker showroom with its original sign
a stately abandoned public bath
one Irish bar one *halal* butcher
churches mosques and storefronts
which used to be
storefronts churches and mosques
When the anthropologists come
with their teaspoons
finding a new layer every six inches
I hope they can dig up the ruins of the
desperate restaurant which featured
Chinese-American-Norwegian Specialties

Now walk over this way, please
Around the corner, just beginning to cook,
are 30,000 Mexicans

Halloween

The second largest retail blowout in the USA
but can it ever regain its immortal apostrophe?
Could Santa Claus still fit into his elfsuit?

My sister, deep in suburban greenery,
says she can't be bothered to keep
running to the door, so
she leaves a basket of candy
on the front porch, with a sign
"Help yourself."
I'd like to try that in Brooklyn.
The first kid to come along
would take all the candy,
the basket, the iron gate, the trash
cans, the doorbell and
the first ten steps of the stoop.
Am I proud of the little bastard?
It helps that he's hypothetical

Record Snowfall

Jaki rested her shovel against a drift.

No more, she told Henry, every muscle aches.

There was a guy across the street, shoveling out the Morrises.

See if he could finish for us, she said. If he can't do it now, ask for his card.

His card? You figure he has a card?

He might have a card. And see if he can do it here or do we have to go to his office.

August 1968

Walking with Jed in the woods near Woodstock along a dirt road that's barely there, a suggestion of road. A lumber road, I think, but what lumber is cut near Woodstock? There are no hearty lumberjacks in the bars, people buy their logs in supermarkets. But there is a hint of road and now, surprise, the sound of a car and then the car itself. A dusty Plymouth with Arkansas plates driven by a man who has a military air even though he's wearing a golf shirt. Says good morning, comments on heat, asks directions. Road must go *somewhere,* I figure, "Keep going, you'll hit Route 212." I don't ask how he got here, none of my business. He thanks me politely, drives about thirty feet, stops, backs up, rolls down his window, looks at my son's curly blond head, says "Boy, get a haircut," rolls up his window, drives off again as though he wasn't the dopey bastard who was lost.

Sentimental Moment Or Why Did the Baguette Cross the Road?

Don't fill up on bread
I say absent-mindedly
The servings here are huge

My son, whose hair may be
receding a bit, says
Did you really just
say that to me?

What he doesn't know
is that when we're walking
together, when we get
to the curb
I sometimes start to reach
for his hand

History by Holes

My mother decided my brother-in-law was
a crook and she cut his face
out of all the old photographs
The head of my first wife also disappeared

So there's the happy table at the wedding
everyone a little smashed and smiling
except the two headless bodies
their hands raising glasses
to pour Champagne down their necks

Too Good

My mother always knew what the matter was
I'm too good, she'd complain
I let people walk all over me
I'm too good

It was a chronic condition: She was
never *merely* good or *pretty* good or
nearly good, not to mention
not good. She was too goddamned
good

And did people take advantage of
this goodness? Of course they did.

They ate the abundant dinners that were
ten times better than the crap they served
and they accepted her exquisite birthday
gifts and did they think she'd ever wear
the cheap junk they tried to
foist off on her, as though she knew
nothing of foisting

But they never got the point
so she had to keep inviting them to
bigger dinners and she had to keep buying
more expensive gifts and
keep showing them
how to wear jewelry

and organize bridge games
and dress like a star

And if she had to keep
hammering away to get her
goodness across
well, that was just too bad

The Big Occasions

She was expecting a surprise party, of course,
so after the dinner for 60 friends all dressed as
water buffalo, he gave her the tickets for the
kayak trip to Tierra del Fuego.

After the surprise party for 50 friends all
dressed as grass and boulders, and the customary
surprise week at the Iwo Jima Hilton,
the plastic surgeon burst out of
the cake, threw her on the rug and
started the complete body renovation.

After the surprise party for 40 friends all
dressed as Manchurian warlords, and a
surprise safari to the Greenland bituminous
mines and the surprise surgery
that de-webbed her toes and added
six inches of muscle to her elbows,
all her children, newly paroled, exploded from
the closets and beat her severely
with bundles of twigs.

Surprise, she whispered, as she sank to
the floor. The children aren't yours,
the guests are carved from ice and
my nose is growing back. Still –
there's something about these big
occasions. It's the other 364 days.

Everybody in New York

I know maybe a dozen words of Yiddish,
about what my Irish and Puerto Rican neighbors know.
(Lenny Bruce said everybody in New York is Jewish
and everybody outside of New York is not Jewish)
but I do know one complete sentence:
"Gae gezinta hae" which sounds like short
division, but actually means "Go in good health"
and *that* sounds like a benediction, but I always
hear it more as "You have embarked on an
idiotic course which you are intent on pursuing
to its utterly disastrous conclusion and no appeal to
reason can dissuade you: therefore, what the hell,
go in good health." Wait —

I know another one: "Z'chub in bood," which
means "I've got you in the bathtub." That is,
"I am hovering above you, fully clad and imposing,
perhaps even armed, and you are naked and shivering
in the bath, staring up helplessly, your genitals shriveled,
your eyes red, your face flushed, your implements
out of reach, as you try to imagine what plan I have
devised for your discomfort or destruction."

Or it may just be that my father had the better
gin rummy hand. It's a language strong for drama,
I think. I have no idea how to express affection in it.

Mysteries of Marriage

Who knows the secrets of someone else's
marriage, she said

We had dinner with them twice a week
for 23 years and now we've heard
(nobody called, we just heard) that she's living
with her aroma therapist and he has a thing for
teenage boys
        Specifically, it's redheaded teenage
boys having sex with fox terriers in
restaurant basements while he, dressed in a sailor suit,
watches from a dark corner
This would make casual sex very hard to come by,
I would think, but maybe it's more of a scene
than I know

We promised ourselves (because who else cared
to know what we thought) that we would not take sides,
that we would stay friends with both of them,
that we would alternate Chinese dinners with
him and vegetarian dinners with her and be nicer
than hell to their new partners, but in fact
we haven't heard a word from either of them
I thought I saw her crouch
behind a mailbox when she saw us coming,
holding hands and skipping as we often do
Everyone thinks we're so goddamn happy

Olives

Donna says olives are packed
in tall narrow jars so
all the olives can see out.

It's not the sort of thing
she would write down, she says
but if I write it down –
and I am clearly the sort of person who
would write it down and in fact
I *have* written it down—
I should give her credit. Well,
maybe I will and maybe I won't.

When I enter New York Hospital
to be carved upon by Dr. Fowler,
several people say "You might get
a good poem out of it, Donna did"
as though we were competing for
the most interesting scar.

I'll show this to her and she'll hand it
back without looking up. Not finished,
she'll say. But of course it is.
Maybe not.

Lunch With Lizzie and Dinner With Donna

1.

Elizabeth and I like it when people say
they can tell we're father and daughter
because of the strong resemblance
since, technically,
she is the daughter of my first wife
by a still earlier marriage out in San Francisco
and her biological father is a tall silent man
from Oklahoma. When this happens
Lizzie gives me a Sly Look from the
corner of her eye (I still call her Lizzie.
You'll have to call her Elizabeth; we're
all grown-ups here). Lizzie's eyes look
Asian, a souvenir of premature birth.
Chinese waiters think she's Korean and
Korean waiters think she's Japanese.
It drives them crazy. Dumb old ladies
used to shout across the sidewalk
"Hey, what's the matter with her eyes?"
But we can't wait for the light to dawn.
We're busy people. I have to go scribble
on things. Lizzie has to ride her bicycle
all over town, her curly hair streaming and
her short legs pumping. There she is,
spinning through the traffic. Watch out
for wilding cabs.

2.

Now Donna is walking with a cane
because she has a bad hip and strangers
(those *same* dumb people thirty years later!)
say "Operation, huh?" and "What did *you*
do to yourself?" Although she says
cabs give her an extra second or two
to reach the curb. Donna is Lizzie's stepmother.
That is, she's my wife. Or Lizzie's late mother's
second ex-husband's second wife. There is another
stepmother out in the Mission district,
wife of the man from Oklahoma,
but she's in her own time zone.
I put my whole family
together out of scraps, Lizzie says.
Donna doesn't like it when I refer to my "first
wife." She says it makes her feel like one
in a series or as though she's lost a race.
But former, ex-, late and then- don't seem much better.
Let's not quibble, not when the streets are choked
with anonymous white trucks, dented and gleaming.
All the drivers are losing it, lowering their horns
and charging wildly into the bicycles and the chugging
walkers and the misty little sedans. I know, I know,
I won't shout back or raise a fist. Just give them a
Mark McGwire swing or two, cane to windshield,
and let's all get across.

Another Town

Misfortune nursed me as her child
and loved me fondly, too
A.P. Carter

every kiss leaves a scar
every caress a bruise

she said
what can I do
with a love like that

love that leaves dents
love that burns your house down
love that kills your cat
love that empties your pockets
love that ruins your digestion
that blunts your perception
that makes you fear the open door
that clouds your memory
bends your fingers back
makes your clothes fit wrong
your confidence crumble
your neighbors sneer
your best friends cry
ego shatter
tongue thicken
brain rot

what can I do
with a love like that

crooked game
only game in town

move

From the Balcony of the Hotel Della Signoria

This is not the real me the real me
has been removed to a museum
and this plaster me
has been put here to stand
in all weather
so tourists can imagine
the warmth of my real thigh

It is not that I really wish to be
a seller of gloves
in a sliver of a shop
on the via Por Santa Maria
I'd just like to slip into his life
for a day or two and out of this
baggy, wrinkled life I brought with me

Does he have trouble with the key
every morning or just on rainy Mondays?
Now who has called him before he's even
got the lights on? His wife, his mother,
the owner—he keeps nodding into
the telephone   The Ponte Vecchio is silent
(gold merchants do not rise early)
but here's sudden color and movement:
a Japanese tour group comes trotting along
at good pace   They pause, they look
and they're off again   I hope his crossword
puzzle book is thick and easy for this long

gray finger of a day

     And you, still asleep on a pile
of your pillows and mine, don't even know
that I went on a journey and now I've returned

I've drunk all my coffee,
now I'm starting on yours

North from Naples

On the train from Naples
miserable honeymooners
from Alabama

Who sold them on this?
The airline lost all their
clothes, waiters keep bringing
them is-that-squid-or-what
and they're not sure whether
they're riding north or south,
the position of the sea
notwithstanding

She talks, he sulks
an American groom
but he is looking forward
to renting one of those scooters
and racing
down the broad boulevards of
where is it they're going, Venice

Cause and Effect

I could triple-tongue a kazoo and
I thought surely that meant bliss
was guaranteed because I could draw a map
of London by memory and trace
the Serpentine with a prehensile
toe enabling me to send back flagons
of burgundy and whole roasted buffalo until
headwaiters wept, but still there was nothing
to be notarized in triplicate and left in a cab
on its way to Brooklyn through the Holland Tunnel
so meanwhile I encourage the trees to grow
tall this time instead of wide
leading to the arrangement of
the prescription bottles as an infield:
but we still give up the seeing-eye hit
(the glyburide can't move to its right)
which is why I came in second for the summer position
and now I'm waiting to be hooked up
and moved from room to room
like furniture

On the Model of Popsicle

Finally, there are the
great questions
And the answers are complex

Is it Fudgicle or Fudgsicle?

It *started* as Fudgicle, then
it was *changed* to Fudgsicle

on the model of Popsicle
to promote order and symmetry
in a melting world

On May 28 of this year
that's one thing I know cold

A Woman Strangles

A woman strangles her fourteen-year-old daughter
to drive out the demons which possess the child.
Very efficient: demons are gone,
a fine demonstration of the role of religion
in everyday life   In fact, she had the assistance of her
sixteen-year-old daughter (who held her sister
down) so this can be considered an instance of
organized religion   If they had just dragged
the girl's body across, say, the Canadian border
they might have established international standing
and qualified themselves as "one of the world's
great religions," thus entitling them to destroy
as many school buses, mud villages, supermarkets,
workers' pubs, tent cities and prime ministers
as their fervor, good book and geography required.

They Turn Unto the Patriarch and the Patriarch is Out to Lunch

A hundred people around the table
Waiter will bring me the check
He'd fight through sumo wrestlers
razor wire and rivers of vomit
to bring me the check
It's this white beard

Brisk walk along the Serpentine
Framed by the sun: young woman in latex
comes running
Glowing sparkling breathing deep
But she smiles
and wishes me a good morning
This ruins everything
It's this white beard

I can still see the faces
in the deck of *Authors*
the intellectual's version of Go Fish
(What an easy game to cheat in!)
I wanted to look like Hawthorne
with egg-yolk yellow hair
never Longfellow with that
long long long white beard
not that long white beard

Celestial Yawning

I assume from the windows
filled with flame
that the sun is setting

I might watch the fireworks
if I happen to be
facing that way

Why stare at an eclipse?
The point of it is that
there's nothing to see

let alone angels

Rapture of the Deep

It really pleases me
when a car signals
a turn

and then
turns

As it veers off
onto the ramp
and disappears into
a particular life

not exactly
like any other
red Ford

Now—to pass the
green van
and lead the highway
to glory

Divisible by Five

A large blonde nurse of a
certain age says to me:
I know you've made a peepee
have you had a poopie?

What did you just say to me?
Hoping it was "There's a steep
drop in the rupee" or "The sleepy
lad felt droopy" but she repeats it
verbatim—slowly
so the addled old fool will understand

and, perception spreading
through the room like a puddle,
I do

Beans

So, last three
red beans
in the can
which didn't get
into the pot—
Now you get
squashed
down the drain
and become part
of Staten Island
landfill
instead of becoming
part of me
Don't fear
It all comes
to the same thing

Mysteries of Dawn and Dusk

Let us consider how to tell
upon waking
if it is getting dark or getting light.
Is your sense of foreboding caused
by dread of the day to come or
dread of the dreams of the day just ended?
Is it merely fear or is it braided with regret?
The clockface is obscured by medicine bottles.
Is it medicine to promote healing or retard
corruption? What of traffic sounds?
Are there alarms or sirens?
Whose coughing do you hear? Are there
dogs? Do the dogs despair or merely hunger?
Do objects in the room have edges
or do they bleed into each other,
silent figures slumped on chairs,
the floorboards a lake of unsupported laundry?
And the quality of the light, judged by
the grayscale—a lightish dark or a darkish light?
Or a third time never lived before?
Does it lift at the corners or is it being nailed down?

Life as Junior High School

You don't think algebra is important
Mrs. Masterson said
but the day will come when you really *need* algebra
You'll be terribly sorry you didn't pay attention
when your life is in ruins and you are a laughingstock

Ha! the joke's on you, lady
Decades have come and gone and
never once, not for a second, did I ever think:
Damn, if I only knew some algebra! Never once,
not for an instant. My hair's turned white and never a
single regret—ha ha ha ha ha

Unless—that moment is still waiting up ahead,
when I'm 92 and trying to remember my shoe size,
my middle name, how many children I have....
And algebra might be the only answer!
I stand in the road, drooling and baffled—
and what's that moving in the fog? Oh god,
it's Mr. Gorman, wearing his devil suit and
waving a chemistry textbook

Grover Cleveland High School, Class of '53

Prelude
I was thrown out of Hebrew school.
For breaking the rabbi's glasses.
Which he was wearing at the time.
While he was trying to drag me
from the room because
I was bouncing a ball. On the wall.
Over the head of the teacher.
While he was leading a class.
This was one of the first overt
demonstrations that I
"lacked the religious sense"
and also prefigured several years of:
"Wipe that smile off your face"
I was terribly pleased.

***

Did anyone ever really masturbate successfully
to a Dagwood and Blondie porno comic?
I suppose so. At fourteen, two pears on a
countertop, certain photographs of sea lions
or a month-old memory of Georgiana Bellisimo
walking out of the girls' room would do the trick
handily. Georgiana's gym shorts still have a pulse.

***

When I was fifteen, my family moved to Queens.
I faced Manhattan and started walking
but too late!
                    Grover Cleveland reached out with his
fat, tobacco-yellow fingers and dragged me to his high school,
a wet woolen building of great girth and heavy moustaches.
Not the French furniture and fine editions of
Thomas Jefferson High School, not the peg-legged
dance rhythms of Stuyvesant or the teachers in powdered
wigs at Washington. In the yearbook to come, many of the girls
aspire to be secretaries, but many others fear to aim that high.
Typists, they write. The boys all want to be firemen, cops and Marines,
they say, but not really. Really, they just want to be mopes and
hang around the locker room forever.

★★★

It's only been half a century
so if you go to the old high school
break the rusty padlock
and feel your way toward
the dripping ruin of the locker room
if you give your eyes a chance
to find shapes in the blackness
there's every reason to think that
way over there in the corner
where the ash of his Lucky Strike
glows and fades and glows
Joe Dooley left fielder and back-up guard
who was never seen in a classroom
or a hallway or a cafeteria
who was always a senior but never a graduate
is still sitting there reading Smokey Stover
and old yellow Dick Young columns

Dooley didn't commit too many
complete sentences but when the coach
didn't name him to the starting five
he said Hey, Hogan —
yer persecutin me on accounta my religion

★★★

Marty and I discovered theater and
foreign movies and also that we
could get served in almost any gay bar
I presumed it was because I looked older,
maybe a little world-weary. Years later,
I realized that any 16-year-old
could probably get served in any gay bar
even if he looked like Quasimodo and
there are probably bars where Quasimodo
would attract special interest. It also
occurred to me that Marty was looking for
more than a few underage beers

★★★

This is for Billy Trowbridge
who knelt down in the crowded
locker room of Grover Cleveland
High School and fixed the zipper
on my fly which had come off
the track May the gods bless Billy
Trowbridge

In our junior year at Grover
Cleveland High School Bob
Johnson who was covered all over

in blond fuzz as though
his mother had never licked him
clean ran away and joined the Marines
He went all through basic training at
Parris Island before they discovered
how old he was and sent him back to
the Ridgewood section of Queens and
Mrs. Greco's Spanish class and Mr.
Boyle's earth science class and
he had still, in his whole life
never crossed the river
into Manhattan

Why have I not run into Nick Carbo
on the subway? We hardly knew each other
at Grover Cleveland High School but
we became pretty friendly on the subway
Every five years without exception
I run into Nick Carbo on the subway
Now suddenly
forty years have gone by and I haven't
run into Nick Carbo anywhere

★★★

During a busy lunch hour, I am walking
down West 47th St., the diamond block,
on my way to the Gotham Book Mart to
see if my new book is in the window,
(so I can stand off to the side and watch
people looking at it) and
a man in a dirty gray uniform is sweeping
the sidewalk in front of a jewelry store while

a horrible blue-haired shrew tells him loudly
and in colorful detail what a useless, incompetent
asshole he is.
                    He is Al Novack, who once held
a knife to my throat in the Grover Cleveland High
School locker room. Do I catch his eye for a
fraction of a second? Maybe, could be. But do
you understand? He is Al Novack who once held
a knife to my throat in the Grover Cleveland
High School locker room and I think
I'll have some wine with lunch.

★★★

Mr. Stone the economics teacher
in some dumb inappropriate connection
said to the class, Alas, poor Yorick
I knew him well, and the class laughed
too heartily. Not me: sixteen, pedantic, in opposition
and unamused   Humor is based on
knowledge, Stone said to me
Horatio, I said
I knew him, *Horatio*

We hate the bad teachers for a lifetime
for their lies, their betrayals, their preening egos
and their cold stupidity
Where would Stone be buried?
There's a use for that skull

★★★

Marian Toshack accuses me of plagiarism
in 11th grade English, although the paper
in question was written in class on a subject
assigned at the beginning of the hour. I have
apparently memorized the entire piece in advance
on the slim chance that she would pick that very topic
Have I memorized a selection of essays on a variety
of topics? Is this seasonal or by category? Do I
offer a choice of voices, a little Francis Bacon, a
little E.B. White? Do I follow MLA style?
What faith the woman has in my abilities!
Does she boast of me to her colleagues?
I have a student so dedicated to his English studies
that he has written and memorized a hundred
essays just on the odd chance that I might
choose one of those subjects.
Yet she glares at me with her hard blue eyes, seemingly
unable to express the deep affection and gratitude she feels.
Meanwhile, not having figured any of this out yet,
I stand in front of her desk, shocked and helpless,
sputtering inarticulate protests.

But right then a door begins to open—the main door
that students aren't allowed to use and I
am out in the air
flying down the steps—two, five, ten
at a time. I am so light!
Heavy gray Grover, goodbye!

The Three Stages of Insomnia

1. Initial

Elio Chacon, Richie Ashburn, Hot Rod
Kanehl, Choo Choo Coleman, Casey
Jones, Yogi Berra, John Berryman, Jesse Gonder,
Jack Fisher, Jeffrey Hunter, Margaret
Thatcher, Home Run Baker, Homer Collier,
Miller Barber, Brewer, Farmer, Snider, Kiner

2. Intermediate

Keith Hernandez, Keith Orpheum, Doc
Gooden, Ray Knight,
Good Night, Sweet Prince, Darryl
Strawberry, John Berryman, Ho Jo,
Ha Jin, John Stearns, Milton
Cross, Hank Sauer, Bob Grimm

3. Terminal

Robin Ventura, Luther Burbank,
Victoria de los Angeles,
Mike Piazza, Piazza Navona, John
Franco, Garcia Lorca, Mike Hampton,
East Hampton, John Ashbery, John Berryman,
Al Leiter, Day Light

Kandinsky: Paintings 198, 199, 200, 201

"The panels have often been interpreted as representing
the four seasons...." Princess Summerfall Winterspring
tears off a page and prepares an abstract for the children
This is not a calendar, they puff

***

She paused briefly before each painting, made some fast entries in
a purple notebook with a much-scribbled-on cover, and moved
to the next painting on her right. I was at the other end of the
gallery, moving left. No one else there this rainy morning. She
asked me for the time and conversation developed. Which one do
you like best? she asked. I don't think I have a favorite, I said, do
you? Oh yes, she said, and led me back to the Kandinskys. See,
she said, it's got a cow and the man in the moon and these birds
and butterflies and this hand reaching up and I think a goat, but I
don't like the mummy.

***

He has not been to school in two weeks
He stands in a corner of the gallery
watching the tourists looking at the Kandinskys
Then he eats lunch Then he goes to the film, any film
Then he watches the people looking at the Pollacks
Then he goes home
The next morning then he comes back

***

in 1961 my apartment in north beach
had split-rattan blinds and kandinsky
posters scotch-taped to the walls
and a table made from a door
and a bricks-and-boards bookcase
and a mattress on the floor
and almost everything was painted
flat black except for the little yellow
desk I bought from good will
and I wrote my first poems sitting there
watching cars curve down
the lombard street hill
with dick partee lying on the couch
behind me reading the chronicle
and rehearsing on his invisible alto
hey man, am I bothering you
no dick, that's okay, it's 2001 now
play some more

Locked

The body like a tenement
bathroom   The tiles loose
the faucets dripping, the rust
stains in the tub, the weak
yellow light
          And the banging on
the door
Hey, you say
Hey, I'm still in here